83

SHORT POEMS

APAR SINGH

Copyright © Apar Singh
All Rights Reserved.

This book has been published with all efforts taken to make the material error-free after the consent of the author. However, the author and the publisher do not assume and hereby disclaim any liability to any party for any loss, damage, or disruption caused by errors or omissions, whether such errors or omissions result from negligence, accident, or any other cause.

While every effort has been made to avoid any mistake or omission, this publication is being sold on the condition and understanding that neither the author nor the publishers or printers would be liable in any manner to any person by reason of any mistake or omission in this publication or for any action taken or omitted to be taken or advice rendered or accepted on the basis of this work. For any defect in printing or binding the publishers will be liable only to replace the defective copy by another copy of this work then available.

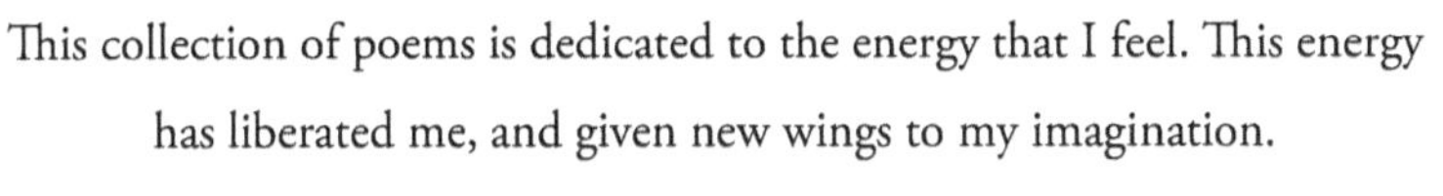

This collection of poems is dedicated to the energy that I feel. This energy has liberated me, and given new wings to my imagination.

It's the energy due to which art exists in this world, and every artist craves for. Like my previous ones, this work too is dedicated to the same heavenly energy.

Contents

Contents

Preface

This is my first short poems collection. I intended to quit poetry, and focus on short stories. But, here I am - guilty! Guess, I can't overlook the fact anymore that poetry comes naturally to me. However, I've tried to keep it short this time.

These poems reflect a lover's state of mind in highs and lows. These are purely one-sided poems, when your love outlasts theirs. I'm no expert on love, life or anything for that matter. I just write what I feel, and if you readers find you can connect with what I say, that makes my work meaningful. Hope you'll enjoy this short, bitter-sweet read!

Prologue

Who am I?
How do I function?
Who are you?
How do you function?
Who are we?
How do we function?
Who we can be?
How will we function?
Who you can be?
How will you function?
Who I can be?
How will I function?

Charms

Her ways and charms,

are out of the world.

There was none before,

There'll be none like her.

1. Cuto-meter

1. Blessings

May my blessings be hers,

And give me all her pain.

None shall dare wrong her,

She won't fight alone again.

2. Cuto-meter

Bring another one please,

This cuto-meter is broken.

Levy the max fine please,

For she charms unspoken.

3. Stars

Stars are stuff of dreams,

How often do we look up?

She embodies all desires,

Does she know her worth?

2. Disclaimer

4. Eyebrows

Today she lifted eyebrows,

And swirled her wine glass.

Never before seen a beauty,

And never seen such class.

5. Disclaimer

Where's the disclaimer?

For someone could die.

Why not say it plainer?

Her ways kill, never lie.

6. Unique

She is a unique piece,

With her ways n tease.

Ducks her head shyly,

With a slow raise sees.

3. Key

7. Except

Every thing I can let go,

Except you only I can't.

Every thing can change,

Love, desire of you can't.

8. Key

You're the key to my real,

And a world that's virtual.

Taken me in entirety total,

You fulfil all that's partial.

9. Requited

A love that's requited,

Agony turned to bliss.

Of murmurs & throbs,

Failures, finally a kiss.

4. Treasure

10. Seducer

She's such a seducer,
An iron lady with guts.
She's such an enticer,
A woman with purpose.

11. Treasure

Where's a real treasure?
I know only one in world.
Fonte of pain & pleasure,
She's unseen & unheard.

12. Won

I know I've angered you,
And yet, won admiration.
I might've pestered you,
And yet, won validation.

5. Worship

13. Tempting

She's above any standards,
I wish to be her amour.
None found so tempting,
Try not to, want her more.

14. Worship

Sure I do worship her,
For how can one not?
I need all her energy,
She never ought not.

15. Jovial

How does she bear me?
I can never understand.
Am oft long-faced man,
She's jovial, a rock band.

6. Left-Right

16. Hand & Shoulder

She patted my shoulder,
So I took, held her hands.
She tapped hand colder,
So I kissed her, no amends.

17. Left-Right

To turn me into right,
We all need a mirror.
Looked into her eyes,
All haze turned clear.

18. Magnum Opus

I have no magnum opus,
Masterpiece aren't words.
There is one golden lotus,
Title only belongs to hers.

7. One

19. Depth

She has a lot of depth,
And I had some reason.
As I drown in her depth,
She can't find a reason.

20. One

One person is enough,
One in a million feeling.
One both good and bad,
One for joys and reeling.

21. Artwork

The result of hard work,
No less than a art work.
Such a joy, my life's perk,
For her oft turn into berk.

8. Transparent

22. Memories

I love your memories,
Badly I despise mine.
Wish make new ones,
If we do get some time.

23. Transparent

She's a mirror, I'm her tain,
She's the stuff, I'm abject.
I only help her reflect back,
Lest me she's transparent.

24. Mine

We can't have a wed-lock,
Though I'd love to be thine.
Give me some of your love,
Also, you can accept mine.

9. Apart

25. Write

Why do I write they ask?
Coz I feel like expressing.
Who makes me feel so?
Only one who's enticing.

26. Apart

Don't add 't' to my name,
Can't anymore stay apart.
On your I place no claim,
Just a place in your heart.

27. Breeze

A soft and soothing breeze,
As lay here in the backyard.
I recall her smile and freeze,
I do wish to be her wild card.

10. Ki

28. Heat Waves

What're these heat waves,
Compared to her swagger.
Think of her & mind sways,
Ways'er no less than dagger.

29. Ki

Which of these Ki is you?
Sumerian Earth goddess.
The vital energy Chinese,
A song that was success?

30. Talk

Let her eyes talk for her,
For she won't say a thing.
I'm content with silence,
To my only hope oft cling.

11. Cop

31. Questioner

I have so many inquiries,
If she could answer them.
How do I get to know her?
Questions un-asked remain.

32. Cop

She cops me sans effort,
Yet she only sets me free.
She cops me so inerrant,
Yet follow now no decree.

33. Differently

Do I see her differently?
Seems happy, yet forlorn.
Why scathe indifferently?
Isn't right to be left alone.

Out-stare

I will out-stare her,

If she gives a chance.

I'll show her the feels,

And what is romance.

12. Long

34. Motion

I've wasted a lot of motion,
Can give her each emotion.
I don't believe in any notion,
Isn't love life's only potion?

35. Long

I long much on rainy days,
To give you my hard long.
I long on these dark nights,
To spread, enter legs long.

36. Wet

In the rains she is wet,
And she is wet inside.
Clothes cling to her body,
My feels cannot subside.

13. Pluck

37. Stay

Ask for more than I say,
Hear me out, then sway.
Feel more than I express,
Stay awhile , before stray.

38. Pluck

I wanna pluck your flower,
Call me, don't care the hour.
And you can take my tower,
Insides of you when I devour.

39. Patient

As I tried to pursue her,
Turned waiter excellent.
And all was at her mercy,
For a change, I'm patient.

14. Coition

40. Haste

Haste makes waste, is said,

Aren't times un-lived sad?

Oxytocin, dopamine dread,

Are feelings un-real, u mad?

41. Coition

All I pray is for her time,

Deities they must listen.

Already have lost much,

Can't wait for the coition.

42. Abstain

She doesn't need abstain,

I'm an open book, laid-back.

And how do I try abstain?

If could spill, front & back.

Heart-Burn

Often give me heart-burn,

But soothe it very less.

For you I go out of turn,

Heart and mind are mess.

15. Kill

43. What

I wonder who what it takes,
For you to understand me.
I live and die for your sakes,
And you always strand me.

44. Kill

I told her that it'll kill me,
She didn't pay any heed.
I'm not her, she's not me,
Which of us other need?

45. Small talk

All we make is small talk,
Couldn't we be a lot more.
It is not a walk in the park,
Alone I lay, ponder ashore.

16. Insecure

46. Insecure

Unsure of why insecure,

We never own anything.

She's not mine to claim,

A-part, fear many-a-thing.

47. Chagrined

Chagrined I felt today,

She threw me out again.

Mind says leave, I stay,

Prior indirect, now plain.

48. Obsession

When bee's in a bonnet,

There's no greater lament.

Obsession takes over me,

Ain't such painful torment.

17. Fear

49. Distances

I yearn walking beside you,
Watching you come and go.
I learnt staying far from you,
That distances gimme a low.

50. Fear

My fear of abandonment,
Made me lose my breath.
Needy & embarrassment,
Angry at betrayal in head.

51. Basic

When you fight for basic,
How far can you really go?
When eyes need LASIK,
How do you jump the row?

18. Texting

52. Awake

How many nights I lay,
Lying awake in my bed.
Numerous times I say,
She never cares a tad.

53. Texting

Don't know if good or bad,
This whole texting scene.
Texts I send drive me mad,
Whether seen or unseen.

54. Meeting

As long we keep waiting,
Able to keep myself sane.
And when we can't meet,
I'm overwhelmed, insane.

19. Who

55. Who

Who helped undressed you,
Was it company or yourself?
Who pulled out your lingerie,
Was it a demon or a goddess?

56. Poor

Ah! the pain of being poor,
There's none greater in world.
Poor can't make love to her,
Impoverished, oft go unheard.

57. Come back

You were with many before,
I have walked in only lately.
I beg you, come back to me,
Open up, talk, why play me?

20. Thunder Storms

58. Money

Sure money can't buy love,
But car, dinner & getaways.
It's a key to treasure's trove,
It's top, down & sideways.

59. Thunder Storms

Thunders strike my heart,
Storms raging in my mind.
Any moment can fall apart,
Love me, and to me be kind.

60. No one

No one knows my pain,
My lover cannot fathom.
Why does she complain,
Am I no one, a random?

21. Damaged

61. Record

I'm a broken record on loop,
A cassette with broken reel.
My emotions beyond recoup,
Wish only if could, myself kill.

62. Damaged

I'm so damaged, can't say,
Think of her night and day.
Wonder with whom she lay,
Such thoughts my soul flay.

63. Test

Who's who now test me,
All suckers do detest me.
Haven't seen the best me,
Until I do it, won't rest me.

22. Out

64. Misery

One person's misery is,

Other one's time of fun.

One person's agony is,

Other one's no concern.

65. Out

Out she goes with him,

Hope not out of my life.

Does she kiss at whim?

My heart with pains rife.

66. Broken

I am so broken, cannot cry,

Discover tears of pain or joy.

My eyes are waterless, dry,

No matter how low or high.

23. Blocked

67. Scary

This morning was scary,
And so was my last night.
She's becoming too wary,
Seeing all in black & white.

68. Blocked

She blocked me tonight,
And unliked all of my pics.
I wanna set things right,
I wonder what she thinks.

69. Break

I wanna shatter my bones,
And break myself tonight.
Drown self in deep waters,
Throw myself from height.

24. Shadow

70. Impure

My thoughts are impure,
How do I even say them?
Mistakes, crazy, haywire,
Hope you can forgive xem.

71. Shadow

Maybe I'm losing her today,
Maybe I'll lose her tomorrow.
Maybe I've lost her yesterday.
Maybe I'll remain her shadow.

72. Unconventional

I was sleep walking then,
We came into others lives.
I don't know why & when,
Unconventionally she rives.

25. Deduce

73. Green Light

Gawping at a red light,
It's already bit too late.
Search for a green light,
Till then all I do is wait.

74. Deduce

It feels like I know you,
And yet, know nothing.
Try to understand you,
I can't deduce nothing.

75. Missing you

Wake up early mornings,
Often sleep light and late.
Checking Whatspp, Insta,
Is this a low or high of fate?

26. Pain

76. Fresh Start

How do I not feel sorry,

For times spent apart.

Can hold hands again?

Let's have a fresh start.

77. Pain

Why I was not there?

For I should'be been.

I blame gods & stars,

My pain must've seen.

78. Tease

I hope life's not a tease,

For I've not had pleasure.

I pin my hopes with ease,

Low or high, need closure.

27. Hate or Love

79. Start-End

My days start, nights end,

With her name on my lips.

Seasons all came and went,

I keep desiring her, amiss.

80. Hate or Love

Not sure if I hate or love it,

The time spent missing you.

Whatever I did or could do,

Nothing comes close to you.

81. Hobby

Missing you's a hobby now,

We know it's come to this.

Oftener you come and go,

Don't I deserve a long kiss?

Deep

My thoughts are deep,

I'm not afraid to admit.

My love you can keep,

I will keep your lament.

28. Un-loved

My fear of being unloved,
I have loved one after long.
It makes me tolerate snub,
I ask myself, do we belong?
My fear to be alone again,
To go back before we met.
The loneliness & the pain,
Is this the return that I get?
My fear of losing her again,
Somehow we've again met.
How do I break these chains?
I shall go all out, than regret.

29. But She

She may get angry,
But never has malice.
She may be proud,
But fire melts her ice.
She may be time-poor,
But of the richest heart.
She may be adamant,
But will gets her to start.
She may be badly hurt,
But never shows scars.
She may reeling in pain,
But heals self too fast.